PRAISE FOR
THE ETHICAL BUSINESS BOOK

"This book has a strong, topical message. Highly recommended."
Fergus Boyd, Director of IT, Red Carnation Hotels

"This book is zen-like in style; Scandi-like in its uncluttered focus; and a clear guide for taking simple, effective action."
Steven Day, Co-founder, Pure Planet

"We all want to be good (or better) – we just don't know where to start. So we never quite get round to doing so. This book helps turn good intentions about ethical business into action. Brilliant."
Mark Earls, author, *Copy, Copy, Copy, I'll Have What She's Having, Herd* and *Creative Superpowers*

"Realistic and practical. I like that it builds on the work of others and focuses on the rewards of 'ethical' behaviour rather than the costs or the risk attached to poor behaviour."
Paul Edwards, Non Executive Director, Creative Nature Superfoods, and Ambassador, Natural History Museum

"Sarah Duncan's *The Ethical Business Book* could not have come at a more timely, or indeed urgent juncture in global politics. Young people everywhere are reminding us that action on the environment is not optional – it's a necessity. This book brings together all aspects of what business must do to keep up – for employees, consumers, shareholders AND communities."
Marjorie Ellis Thompson, co-author, *The New Brand Spirit*

"This is timely. CSR, sustainability and ethics are becoming mainstream. All businesses need an action plan for the new market reality. *The Ethical Business Book* is their guide. Invaluable."

Hamish Pringle, co-author, *Brand Spirit* with Marjorie Thompson and *Brand Manners* with William Gordon

"It is a comprehensive collection of ideas to help organisations move to a more ethical and sustainable future."

Mark Smith, Director, simple truth

"The message here is clear and not just for CEOs. I've seen myself, working with large organisations, how people in the so called 'middle ground' can affect change. It all starts with one conscious thought. This book is the next iteration of what responsibility looks like in business."

Kaye Taylor, Founder, SK Chase Ltd

"This is a brilliant tool for all business owners who are committed to running an ethical and sustainable company but don't know where to start. Sarah breaks it down into bite-sized chunks and gives you the tools to start protecting not only your profits but both your people and the planet."

Ceri Tinley, MD, Consensio Chalets

"Clear and easy to read. Lots of useful and practical things to think about to set you on an ethical journey."

Kate Thompson, Director of Marketing, Trains & Cruises, Belmond

Published by
LID Publishing Limited
The Record Hall, Studio 204,
16-16a Baldwins Gardens,
London EC1N 7RJ, UK

info@lidpublishing.com
www.lidpublishing.com

A member of:

BPR
Business Publishers Roundtable

www.businesspublishersroundtable.com

Printed in Latvia by Jelgavas Tipogrāfija

ISBN: 978-1-912555-58-1

Cover and page design: Caroline Li

THE ETHICAL BUSINESS BOOK

50 WAYS YOU CAN HELP PROTECT PEOPLE, THE PLANET AND PROFITS

SARAH DUNCAN

MADRID | MEXICO CITY | LONDON
NEW YORK | BUENOS AIRES
BOGOTA | SHANGHAI | NEW DELHI

CONTENTS

AUTHOR'S NOTE ON SUSTAINABILITY   1
INTRODUCTION   2

PART 1: PROTECTING PROFITS
1. THE ONLY WAY IS ETHICS   8
2. CSR HAS MOVED ON   10
3. IF YOU'RE GOING TO CHANGE, CHANGE FOR GOOD   14
4. EVERYONE'S GOT TO START SOMEWHERE   18
5. WHAT'S YOUR MORAL PURPOSE?   20
6. IT'S ALL ABOUT THE TRIPLE BOTTOM LINE   24
7. MISSION STATEMENTS NEED MEANING   28
8. BUILD THE FIRM OF THE FUTURE   30
9. FORGET THE A TEAM, BRING IN THE B TEAM   32
10. WHO ARE YOU PROTECTING?   34

PART 2: PROTECTING EMPLOYEES
1. WHY SHOULD ANYONE WORK HERE?   40
2. ADOPTING A CONSCIOUS CULTURE   44
3. EMBRACE DIVERSITY   46
4. FIND YOUR PERSONAL PURPOSE   48
5. IS YOUR TEAM DYSFUNCTIONAL?   50
6. MAKE WAY FOR THE MAVERICKS   54
7. FIND YOUR SOCIAL INTRAPRENEURSHIP   56
8. THE AGE OF THE ECO-LEADERS   58
9. HOW TO AVOID A FIZZLE-OUT   62
10. MY EMPLOYEE ACTION PLAN   64

PART 3: PROTECTING CUSTOMERS
1. THOU SHALT LOOK AFTER CUSTOMERS   72
2. COULD CONSCIOUS CONSUMERISM BE KILLING YOUR BUSINESS?   74
3. FEED YOUR CUSTOMERS' PASSIONS   76

4.	WALK IN YOUR CUSTOMERS' SHOES	78
5.	TALK TO YOUR BIGGEST FANS	80
6.	IS ANYONE REALLY LISTENING?	82
7.	TIME TO PAY IT FORWARD?	86
8.	ARE YOUR CUSTOMERS VAGUELY LOYAL OR FULLY COMMITTED?	88
9.	MAKE WAY FOR THE MATURING MILLENNIALS	90
10.	MY CUSTOMER ACTION PLAN	92

PART 4: PROTECTING THE PLANET

1.	THERE IS NO PLANET B	100
2.	REDUCING YOUR CARBON FOOTPRINT	104
3.	CONSERVING ENERGY	106
4.	CONSERVING WATER	110
5.	NOT ALL WASTE IS BORN EQUAL	112
6.	IS YOUR BUSINESS A RIVER OR LAKE?	114
7.	GREENING YOUR SUPPLY CHAIN	116
8.	ARE YOU AN ECO- OR EGO-WARRIOR?	120
9.	OVERCOMING THE RESISTORS	122
10.	MY PLANET ACTION PLAN	124

PART 5: ETHICAL MARKETING

1.	MARKETING – FROM MANIPULATION TO AUTHENTICITY	132
2.	THE NEW PRINCIPLES OF ETHICAL MARKETING	134
3.	GREENWASHING WON'T WASH	136
4.	TOO LITTLE, TOO TRIUMPHANT, TOO LATE?	138
5.	STORYDOING AND DATATELLING	140
6.	BOGOF REINVENTED – BUY ONE, GIVE ONE FREE	144
7.	NAVIGATING THE COMPETITION	146
8.	ARE YOU AN ETHICAL GAME CHANGER?	148
9.	MINIMUM EFFORT, MAXIMUM RETURN	150
10.	THE INFINITE ETHICAL LOOP	154

FINAL WORD	158
RESOURCES AND FURTHER READING	164
ACKNOWLEDGMENTS	167
ABOUT THE AUTHOR	168

FOR OTHER TITLES
IN THE SERIES...

CONCISE
ADVICE
LAB

SMALL BOOKS: BIG IDEAS

CLEVER CONTENT, DYNAMIC IDEAS, PRACTICAL
SOLUTIONS AND ENGAGING VISUALS –
A CATALYST TO INSPIRE NEW WAYS OF THINKING
AND PROBLEM-SOLVING IN A COMPLEX WORLD

conciseadvicelab.com

AUTHOR'S NOTE ON SUSTAINABILITY

It will not escape some people's notice that this book, which features the importance of environmental sustainability, creates its own carbon footprint. However, in order to get these important messages across to a wider audience, I felt I needed to make a compromise. This will be a recurring theme in the book.

I believe it is unrealistic to think that businesses (and humans) can adopt ethically *perfect* behaviours overnight. Businesses still need to conduct business – make things, distribute things, communicate things. This book is about challenging every aspect of your business (and indeed life) to see where you can make a difference.

I have made a donation to ClimateCare.org to offset the production of this book. This is an organization that allows businesses to carbon offset their activities and support amazing carbon-reduction projects worldwide.

And, in the spirit of Time to Pay It Forward (see Part 3.7), for every 100 copies of this book sold, I will give ten business or educational books (including others from the LID Concise Advice Series) to worthy causes.

My hope is that if all of us make changes where possible, the overall impact can be significant.

"You can't go back and change the beginning, but you can start where you are and change the ending."

C S Lewis

INTRODUCTION

DOING THE RIGHT THING DOESN'T HAVE TO MEAN LOWER PROFITS

While it's unrealistic to think a company can become fully sustainable overnight, all organizations can begin moving in the right direction.

This book guides you along the path to becoming a better business – for you, your people and the world we live in.

It will help you discover your moral purpose and create a mission that engages employees, inspires customers and helps protect the planet – proving that doing good and making money are not incompatible.

The latest evidence shows that more thoughtful business practice is highly commercial. Your ethical journey should become central to your company's communications strategy (internal and external), helping to set you apart from your competition.

But you can only be ethical in your marketing and communications if you have business integrity. A company does not have to be perfect, but it does need to be honest about the efforts it is making to become a better business – assuming that is what it is striving to do.

Ethical practices must be supported from the top down to be genuine and become a true part of a company's culture.

If you are a business owner or leader, this book will provide you with the tools to start making a difference. If you work for an organization that needs change, this book will give you the ammunition you need to lobby the decision makers and present a robust case for adopting a more ethical approach to the business.

Some sections of the book are quite detailed, but this is not intended to be preachy or holier than thou. It takes time to appreciate all the areas where improvements can be made, and some are easier to address than others. The intention is to help everyone make a move in the right direction – where you take it is your call.

Note: I have drawn on the insights of a number of books and papers on this subject. Sources have been kept as brief as possible in the main text, but more details can be found in the Resources and Further Reading section at the back.

> *"We cannot solve our problems with the same thinking we used when we created them."*
> Albert Einstein

Business practice has come a long way in recent times. The rise of social media has resulted in the demise of big companies simply pushing products at people (at least in the traditional sense). The power now lies more in the hands of consumers.

We look to our peers and influencers to guide our purchasing, not to the advertising copy.

False marketing claims are quickly exposed. And bad service is magnified by social sharing. Customers are demanding transparency, and exposure to behind the scenes of corporations. Companies are now required to tell their story or find their 'narrative'.

The importance to both customers and employees of being associated with higher ethical practices has never been greater and will continue to be a differentiator for decision-making.

So, simply put, acknowledging and responding to this market dynamic will protect your long-term profits.

IN THIS PART we will start by exploring the benefits of being more ethical, and then look at how a company can get started – developing a greater moral purpose, robust business model and engagement plans.

PART ONE

- HAPPY PEOPLE
- HEALTHY PLANET
- HIGHER PROFITS

BAD BUSINESS •
OUTDATED VALUES •
ONE-WAY MARKETING •

PROTECTING PROFITS

1. THE ONLY WAY IS ETHICS

It is now widely accepted that businesses have responsibilities beyond simply making profit. But there are many chief financial officers who would prefer to ignore the moral debate.

So it's important at the very start to make both the ethical *and* the financial point.

The case for adopting more ethical and sustainable business practices is a strong one, which includes driving long-term revenue, reducing costs, and managing risk.

Here are some compelling commercial reasons to support ethical change.

ENHANCED (LONG-TERM) REVENUES	Companies perceived as being socially responsible are rewarded with extra, more satisfied and loyal customers. Perceived irresponsibility can drive customers away.
	Similarly, businesses with ethical agendas will seek out like-minded suppliers and partners that share their principles.
	Employees are also more attracted to and committed to companies perceived as having a moral purpose.
REDUCED COSTS	Sustainable behaviour can reduce costs as it helps in saving energy, reducing waste and cutting out inefficiencies.
MANAGED RISK AND UNCERTAINTY	Voluntarily committing to ethical business practices can, in turn, steal a march on future legislation.
IMPROVED MARKETING AND COMMUNICATION	Companies with authentic and compelling stories to tell gain greater trust and engagement with customers.

To what extent do the most senior people in your business agree with these principles?

2. CSR HAS MOVED ON

Traditional Corporate Social Responsibility (CSR) mainly covers what is generally accepted as decent business behaviour required by society – legally and economically. Business ethics can be said to begin where the law ends. It's primarily concerned with those issues not covered by law and therefore up for interpretation.

Discussion about the ethics of particular business practices (and pressure from stakeholders and society) can eventually lead to changes in the law but, in many cases, it falls to the company's moral compass.

This pyramid illustrates the difference between a company's responsibilities in terms of what is required by society, as opposed to what is expected or desired.

Ethical responsibility may be expected by society, but it falls to the ethical company to do the right thing, because they are not obliged to do so legally.

At the top, philanthropy is by no means a responsibility, but it is highly desirable and, in many societies, much needed.

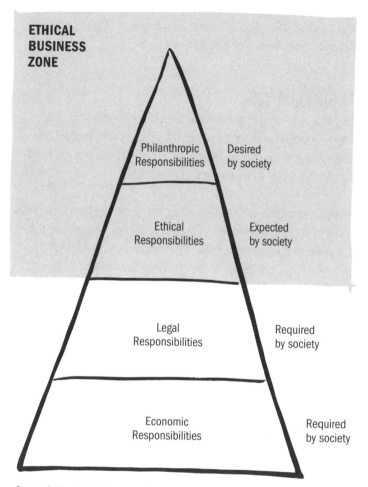

ETHICAL BUSINESS ZONE

Philanthropic Responsibilities	Desired by society
Ethical Responsibilities	Expected by society
Legal Responsibilities	Required by society
Economic Responsibilities	Required by society

Source: *Business Ethics* (Crane & Matten) – *A B Carroll's Four Part CSR Model*

The way companies prioritize different levels of ethical behaviour depends on their overall strategy.

TRADITIONAL CSR

This is a long-standing approach to social responsibility, still widely adopted around the world. It considers CSR as part of a strategy where a company generates its profits without too much consideration for wider societal expectations.

However, once the profit is generated, the company then distributes some of the value created to projects, activities and causes that are important to stakeholders. These activities will ultimately enhance the wider image of the company and bolster its brand identity. Ethical behaviour is therefore 'bolted on'. In Carroll's four-part model, activity for these companies is mostly about philanthropy (Philanthropic Responsibilities).

INTRODUCING THE NEW BUSINESS ETHICS

Modern ethical businesses promote responsible behaviour as an opportunity to generate profits while at the same time living up to expectations of society. Rather than unilaterally dishing out money, they work with stakeholders to understand their interests and expectations. Ethical and sustainable behaviour for these companies is integral, or 'built in' to their core business.

Traditional CSR is now regarded as the old way – making a profit and then doing something responsible with it. The new way builds ethical purpose into the company at the beginning of the financial year, not the end.

	TRADITIONAL CSR	BUSINESS ETHICS
FOCUS	Risk	Reward
DRIVER	Image, Brand, Public Acceptance	Performance, Markets, Products, Integrity
RELATION TO BOTTOM LINE	No direct contribution	Integral goal: High ethics = value creation Purpose = profit
RESPONSIVENESS	Reactive	Proactive
EMPHASIS	Ethical behaviour is bolt-on	Ethical behaviour is built-in

3. IF YOU'RE GOING TO CHANGE, CHANGE FOR GOOD

Change for good represents a shift in thinking and practice across all business and involves a 'systems' as well as 'personal' transformation.

The book *Sustainable Business: A One Planet Approach* (Jeanrenaud, Jeanrenaud & Gosling) powerfully outlines the shifts needed for a company to work toward becoming a more ethical and sustainable business.

Area	Shift From:	To:
ADVERTISING	Creating consumer demand and fuelling consumerism.	Accountable and responsible advertising that discloses product origin, content, life span and disposal.
CAPITAL	Exclusive focus on financial and manufactured capital.	Focus that includes human, social and natural capital.
CONSUMPTION	A culture of individual hyper-consumerism.	Mindful consumption.
ENERGY	A reliance on fossil fuels and power supplies managed by big utilities companies.	Renewable energy resources.
GOVERNANCE	20th century models of shareholder capitalism.	New models of stakeholder capitalism.
INNOVATION	Centrally controlled, incremental, inward-looking innovation processes.	Building innovation ecosystems.

Area	Shift From:	To:
LABOUR	Labour merely as a factor of production in which work is exchanged for money.	Fostering entrepreneurship and encouraging creative and purposeful work.
LEADERSHIP	Individual 'heroic' leadership styles.	Leading through building commitment and engagement.
METRICS	The financial bottom line and quarterly reporting.	Measuring what matters and new metrics of success – such as the triple bottom line.
MINDSETS	Silos and ego.	Systems and eco.
NATURE	Conquering nature.	'Celebrating diversity' and 'learning from the natural world'.
OWNERSHIP	Shareholder models of ownership.	Different ownership models with alternative power and authority structures, pay scales and metrics of performance.
PLACE	Globalization of trade.	Building local living economies.

Area	Shift From:	To:
PRODUCTION	Sourcing the cheapest supplies possible.	Sustainable supply chain management.
PURPOSE	Exclusive focus on making profits for shareholders.	Achieving profits with a social purpose. The recognition that doing good and making money are not incompatible.
RELATIONSHIPS	Exclusive focus on competition.	Working in long-term alliances, and collaborating with investors, consumers and policymakers.
SELF	Focus on sustainability problems 'out there'.	Involving the personal and inner dimensions of social change 'in here' or change from the 'inside out'.
TECHNOLOGY	Mass production, stockpiling and global transportation of goods.	Decentralized production on demand at a local level.
VALUES	Top-down, competitive culture.	Caring, sharing, collaborating and serving the community. From 'me' to 'we'.

4. EVERYONE'S GOT TO START SOMEWHERE

So now we have raised some of the issues in relation to ethical business, here's a basic audit to use as a starting point to highlight your current areas of strengths and weaknesses.

Complete it with your colleagues, as a team or by yourself and use the answers to get the conversation started. 18 yes answers = full marks; 9 = work to be done; 0-8 = serious work to be done.

COMPANY APPROACH

Y/N

The CEO openly supports and prioritizes sustainability and ethical behaviour.

Sustainability is specifically included in the company's mission statement and/or brand values.

The company's business model is designed to benefit people, the planet and profits.

EMPLOYEE ENGAGEMENT AND DIVERSITY

Employees are given opportunities to get involved in environmental and ethical initiatives.

The company takes care of its people by paying a fair (living) wage and related benefits (such as wellness programmes).

Underrepresented groups (women, minorities, LGBTQ, individuals with disabilities) are represented at ALL levels of the business.

ENVIRONMENTAL RESPONSIBILITY
Y/N

The company has specific energy- and water-saving policies.

Recycling is given priority and employees are trained on proper sorting procedures.

Employees are incentivized to take public transport or bike to work rather than drive.

SUPPLY CHAIN AND PROCUREMENT

Preference is given to suppliers with a commitment to social and environmental sustainability.

Preference is given to suppliers who are local.

Environmentally preferable purchasing is set up for paper products, cleaning products and reusable items.

COMMUNITY

The company has a community service policy and encourages employee volunteerism.

The company has a charitable giving policy and makes donations to nonprofit organizations.

The company supports and/or sponsors local events and organizations.

METRICS

The company tracks its energy and water usage, waste generation and carbon footprint.

Sustainability goals have been established and communicated throughout the organization.

The company's sustainability practices have been certified by an independent, third-party organization.

5. WHAT'S YOUR MORAL PURPOSE?

At the heart of establishing the wider moral purpose of your business is the recognition that doing good and making money are not incompatible.

Your purpose resides in the intersection of your strengths, your passions, the company's impact and the rewards you can generate.

Knowing what intrinsically motivates your people, what you're built to do better than anyone else, and where you can deploy that passion and talent to serve a need or solve a problem in the world is extremely powerful.

And the statistics support the importance of this: 81% of US millennials say a successful company needs a genuine purpose that resonates with prople.*

This matrix is from the book *Conscious Capitalism Field Guide* (Sisodia, Henry, Eckschmidt) and provides an excellent framework for establishing where your moral purpose is or should be.

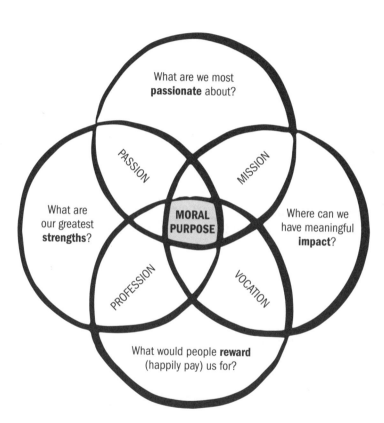

1. **What is our business's greatest strength? What do we have the potential to be the best at in the world?**

2. **What are we most passionate about? What do we love the most about what we do?**

3. **Where can we have the most meaningful impact? Which big problems or needs in the world are we capable of solving?**

4. **What would people reward us for? What products and services would our customers happily pay for (maybe even a little more if we could deliver them in a more ethical fashion)?**
   Note: 73% of US millennials are willing to pay extra for sustainable offerings*

By answering these questions diligently and honestly, a company can get considerably closer to defining its moral purpose and working out what specific actions are needed to enact it.

Do not write formulaic or glib answers to these vital questions. Dedicate sufficient time to the task (I would recommend a full-day workshop).

When all four questions have satisfactory answers, work out how they intersect to generate your overall moral purpose.

* See Make Way for the Maturing Millennials (Part 3.9).

6. IT'S ALL ABOUT THE TRIPLE BOTTOM LINE

The triple bottom line (a term first coined by sustainability thought leader John Elkington) is a business model that consists of not just healthy profits, but high business integrity and environmental sensitivity – resulting in both successful business strategy and moral business practice.

Juggling the commercial and moral imperatives of people, the planet and profit needs time and thought to get right. It does, however, provide the company with the best platform for future responsible business development and all the associated benefits.

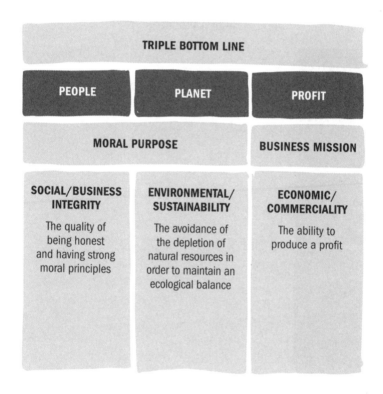

TRIPLE BOTTOM LINE

PEOPLE	PLANET	PROFIT
MORAL PURPOSE		BUSINESS MISSION
SOCIAL/BUSINESS INTEGRITY	**ENVIRONMENTAL/ SUSTAINABILITY**	**ECONOMIC/ COMMERCIALITY**
The quality of being honest and having strong moral principles	The avoidance of the depletion of natural resources in order to maintain an ecological balance	The ability to produce a profit

Start by developing individual statements of intent covering the triple bottom line: people, planet and profit.

INDIVIDUAL STATEMENTS OF INTENT	
MORAL PURPOSE	
PEOPLE	
PLANET	

BUSINESS MISSION

PROFIT

7. MISSION STATEMENTS NEED MEANING

Now that you have your individual statements of intent, you are ready to create (or revisit) your overall company mission statement – using the framework on the opposite page.

Completing this exercise is not something that should be knocked out in an hour or so. It requires proper care and attention from the senior leadership team. Buy-in and ownership really must come from the top.

We have a responsibility to our shareholders to deliver
(business mission or economic statement) ......

whilst (moral purpose statement/s) ....

8. BUILD THE FIRM OF THE FUTURE

Let us recap the main factors that need to be considered to become an ethical business of the future:

	FIRM OF THE PAST	FIRM OF THE FUTURE
BENEFICIARIES	Shareholders	Stakeholders
BOTTOM LINE	Single financial bottom line	Triple bottom line People, Planet, Profits
COMMUNITIES	Corporate Social Responsibility	Ethical business practice: Creating shared value Social enterprise Building community
OPERATIONS	Linear: take-make-waste	Circular: closed loop

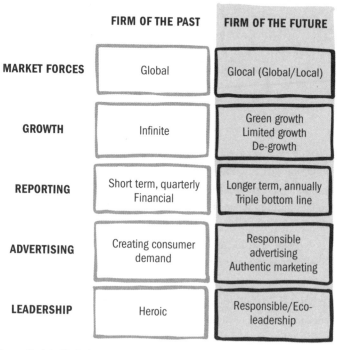

	FIRM OF THE PAST	**FIRM OF THE FUTURE**
MARKET FORCES	Global	Glocal (Global/Local)
GROWTH	Infinite	Green growth Limited growth De-growth
REPORTING	Short term, quarterly Financial	Longer term, annually Triple bottom line
ADVERTISING	Creating consumer demand	Responsible advertising Authentic marketing
LEADERSHIP	Heroic	Responsible/Eco- leadership

Source: *Sustainable Business: A One Planet Approach* (Jeanrenaud, Jeanrenaud, Gosling)

9. FORGET THE A TEAM, BRING IN THE B TEAM

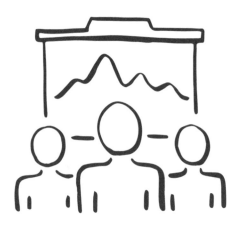

Many companies have a CSR policy that covers elements of charitable giving, community engagement and some degree of environmental sensitivity, but that fails to acknowledge or respond to the fact that the business as a whole does more harm than good.

If you really want to take your ethical journey seriously, bringing in specialists is the way forward.

Certified B Corporations are a movement of businesses that meet the highest standards of verified social and environmental performance, public transparency and legal accountability to balance profit and purpose.

Via the B Corp assessment, you can properly find out how your company performs against dozens of best practices. Taking the assessment alone will be a valuable, eye-opening experience for your company and will help you discover ways to improve.

If you decide to go for certification, you will join an ever-growing group of businesses that believe society's most challenging problems cannot be solved by government and nonprofits alone. By harnessing the power of business, B Corps use profits and growth as a means to a greater end: positive impact for their employees, communities and the environment.

To view the process for your business, see assessment criteria and download guides and checklists, visit bcorporation.net.

There are other industry- or sector-specific bodies that can provide guidance, best practices and accreditation.

For example, in the food service industry, there is the Sustainable Restaurant Association (thesra.org) that offers a comprehensive framework that covers sourcing, society and the environment.

10. WHO ARE YOU PROTECTING?

Before we start looking in more detail at the planet and its resources, the next two parts focus on people.

Businesses need people. They need customers to buy products; employees to make and deliver the goods; suppliers to provide materials and backup; investors and shareholders to keep them afloat; and a loyal community to support their endeavours. Without a healthy stakeholder group, businesses cannot flourish.

When was the last time you thought about each of these groups?

How can you implement initiatives to strengthen your relationships with them and become a better business?

Make a note here of all your stakeholders and keep them in mind as you work through the following sections.

EMPLOYEES

CUSTOMERS

SUPPLIERS

COMMUNITY

SHAREHOLDERS

PROFITS RECAP

1. Start by reviewing the potential benefits to your business of becoming more ethical and sustainable
2. Consider your current CSR policies and how to become a truly ethical business
3. Look at all the aspects of the business that could change
4. Conduct an initial mini-audit to expose main areas of opportunity
5. Brainstorm your company's moral purpose
6. Consider your ultimate goals in relation to your people, the planet and profits – the triple bottom line
7. Combine these to form a new company mission statement with meaning
8. Contrast the firm of the past with that of the future and draw up an action plan
9. Decide if you want to work toward accreditation and build this into your plan
10. Work through your stakeholder list and create a clear understanding of all the people who are invaluable to your business and need to be considered

ETHICAL THOUGHTS

"In looking for people to hire, you look for three qualities: integrity, intelligence and energy. And, if they don't have the first, the other two will kill you."

Warren Buffett

No business can be successful without good people. And good people gravitate toward good businesses.

By 2025, 75% of the workforce will be millennials – a group that will often refuse to work for companies if they are unconvinced of their ethical credentials.

As a result, companies with dubious or questionable ethical stances will fail to attract the top talent they require.

Other statistics show that highly motivated and engaged employees will:

- Generate 43% more revenue and 12% higher productivity
- Take five fewer sick days a year per team member
- Be 87% less likely to leave

Source: Engaging for success: enhancing performance through employee engagement (Macleod Report).

And as we shall see in this section, meaning and purpose play a major part in employee motivation and engagement.

IN THIS PART we will focus on how to develop your new ethical business approach to attract and retain great and diverse talent.

PART TWO

- HIGHER PURPOSE
- WELLNESS
- DIVERSITY

STRESS •
LACK OF PROSPECTS •
BULLYING •

PROTECTING EMPLOYEES

1. WHY SHOULD ANYONE WORK HERE?

Every company wants to attract the best talent, so start by asking yourself:

Why should anyone want to work for your organization?

Here are some great reminders of what makes a good company culture, from the book *Why Should Anyone Work Here?* (Goffee & Jones). A full staff survey example is also available at: ethicalbusinessblog.com.

If the answer is 'no' to any of these questions, then use the box on the right to propose remedies to address the situation.

CRITICAL AREAS	REMEDIES
DIFFERENCE: Does the company let people be themselves? Y/N	
RADICAL HONESTY: Does the company let people know what's really going on? Y/N	

CRITICAL AREAS	REMEDIES
EXTRA VALUE: Does the company magnify peoples' strengths? **Y/N**	
AUTHENTICITY: Does the company stand for something more than just shareholder value? **Y/N**	

CRITICAL AREAS	REMEDIES
MEANING: Does the company make the work make sense? Y/N	
SIMPLE RULES: Does the company make the rules clear and apply them equally to everyone? Y/N	

2. ADOPTING A CONSCIOUS CULTURE

According to the book *Conscious Capitalism Field Guide* (Sisodia, Henry, Eckschmidt), when you walk into an organization, you can feel the difference between a 'conscious' business and a traditional one, and this is down to culture.

There are many books and approaches surrounding company culture. This book promotes the TACTILE approach – an acronym representing seven qualities for companies to consider.

- A high degree of **trust** permeates conscious businesses internally and externally with all stakeholders
- **Authenticity** is essential to build trust
- Feeling cared for and **caring** for others are core human needs
- Conscious cultures are **transparent**, because there's little to hide
- A strict adherence to truth-telling and fairness are at the heart of business **integrity**
- A continual desire to **learn** helps businesses successfully evolve
- Hire people with a strong fit to your company's culture and **empower** them to act intelligently and thoughtfully

T Trust

A Authenticity

C Caring

T Transparency

I Integrity

L Learning

E Empowerment

3. EMBRACE DIVERSITY

The best businesses benefit from a dynamic and diverse mix of people. Diversity and inclusion are now, quite rightly, hot topics in business. It often starts with internal debate on team diversity but should also extend to customer awareness and marketing sensitivity.

Like many of the big and important ethical business initiatives, this will require expert focus to enact properly and with full integrity. However, the questions here can help start a healthy debate.

Think carefully about who you want to have answer these questions, and who should be involved in the subsequent debate.

Try to avoid the cliché of Male, Pale and Stale (or Yale) – an all-too-common scenario of male-orientated boardroom decision making with no representation from minority groups.

When was the last time the company conducted a diversity and inclusion audit?

Does your company genuinely celebrate differences? Can you give examples?

Are you proud of the diversity in your company – including gender, race, sexual orientation, disability, age and religion?

Are each of these groups represented at ALL levels of the business?

Are there currently cliques and silos within the business?

Does the company encourage open debate on diversity?

Does your company have a Diversity Manager or 'go-to' person for diversity matters/concerns?

Do your marketing materials correctly reflect the diversity of your employees and customers?

4. FIND YOUR PERSONAL PURPOSE

Nothing gets done if no one can be bothered. And lack of moral purpose in business leads to reduced motivation. In his book *Drive*, Daniel Pink boils the essence of motivation down to three crucial elements, the third of which is Purpose.

1. **AUTONOMY** is the desire to direct our own lives.
   Example question: Are people allowed to get on with their work uninterrupted and be themselves?

2. **MASTERY** is the urge to get better and better at something that matters.
   Example question: Are people given sufficient training, support and tools to make them competent and confident in their work?

3. **PURPOSE** is the yearning to do what we do in the service of something larger than ourselves.
   Example question: Is the (moral) purpose of individuals aligned well with that of the team, department, or company?

Empowerment and training can cover the first two, but a strong company moral purpose is required for the third.

If all three components are true, then high motivation levels will follow. Diligent, ethical companies will need metrics that measure whether all this is coming together for the overall good.

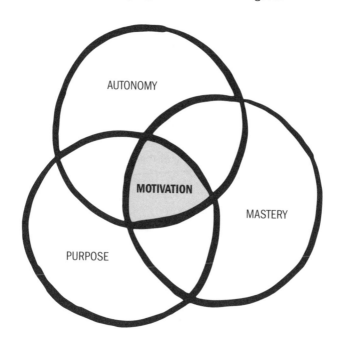

There can be various levels to such an exercise:
- Ask individuals to do it
- Ask teams to do it
- Ask the whole company to do it

Compare the results. Then identify and discuss inconsistencies.

5. IS YOUR TEAM DYSFUNCTIONAL?

Good businesses need functioning teams. There are five dysfunctions that can ruin the effectiveness and cohesion of any team, as outlined in the book *The Five Dysfunctions of a Team*, by Patrick Lencioni.

Each dysfunction builds on the previous, making it even more difficult to isolate just one issue in a team. The foundation, however, needs to be trust – one of the most important elements of ethical business practice.

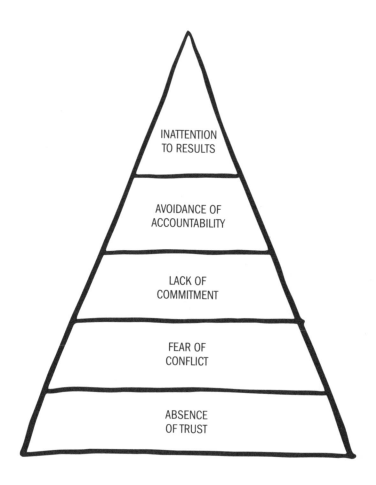

INATTENTION
TO RESULTS

AVOIDANCE OF
ACCOUNTABILITY

LACK OF
COMMITMENT

FEAR OF
CONFLICT

ABSENCE
OF TRUST

So, starting from the bottom (or foundation) of the pyramid and moving to the top, the important points are:

1. **ABSENCE OF TRUST.** Teams that are not open about mistakes and weaknesses make it impossible to build trust.

2. **FEAR OF CONFLICT.** Teams that lack trust are incapable of engaging in unfiltered debate. Instead, they resort to veiled discussions and guarded comments.

3. **LACK OF COMMITMENT.** Without having aired their opinions in open debate, team members rarely, if ever, buy in or commit to decisions.

4. **AVOIDANCE OF ACCOUNTABILITY.** Without committing to a clear plan of action, even the most focused people fail to call their peers to account.

5. **INATTENTION TO RESULTS.** Failure to hold one another accountable creates an environment where team members put their individual needs above the team.

So, in conclusion:

- Trust comes from overcoming invulnerability and admitting to weaknesses
- Constructive conflict needs to replace artificial harmony
- Creating commitment means removing ambiguity
- Accountability involves raising low standards
- Inattention to results can be addressed by removing status and ego issues

An assessment of this type has the capacity to expose uncomfortable deficiencies in teams, so think carefully about the implications and who should be involved before proceeding.

6. MAKE WAY FOR THE MAVERICKS

You need brilliant people to run a great business – particularly if you are to effectively juggle the needs of society, the planet and the bottom line. A handful of star performers can create disproportionate amounts of value for their organizations. These are exactly the types of employees looking to work for a company with a greater moral purpose, so attracting and retaining them is crucial.

But although the 'clever ones' can be brilliant, they can also be difficult. Their cleverness is central to their identity; their skills are not easily replicated; they know their worth; they ask difficult questions; they are organizationally savvy; they are not impressed by hierarchy; they expect instant success; they want to be connected to other clever people; and they won't thank you.

They also take pleasure in breaking the rules. They can be oversensitive about their projects and are never happy about the review process.

So traditional leadership approaches are often ineffective. Instead, bosses need to tell them what to do (not how to do it), earn their respect with expertise (not pull rank with a job title), and provide 'organized space' for their creativity.

There is also an almost endless need to restate the company's moral purpose and verify that it aligns with what mavericks are being asked to do. Failure to do this will usually result in them pointing out the gap between strategy and execution.

Here are some dos and don'ts.

DO ...	DON'T ...
Earn their respect with expertise, not a job title	Use hierarchy
Tell them what you want done	Tell them how to do it
Provide boundaries – organized space for creativity	Create bureaucracy
Give them time	Interfere
Give them recognition (amplify their achievements)	Give frequent feedback
Encourage failure and maximize learning	Train by rote (they are already highly skilled)
Talk straight	Intentionally deceive

Source: *Clever* (Goffee & Jones)

7. FIND YOUR SOCIAL INTRAPRENEURSHIP

As introduced in the book *WEconomy* (Kielburger, Branson, Kielburger), purpose is not a singular task reserved for the higher-ups. Anyone can achieve purpose at work, and everyone should try, since it benefits an eager employee as much as it does the business.

The book promotes the idea that anyone in an organization can step up and volunteer to get involved or lead cause-related activities – like the company's community day, charity event or diversity programme. This in turn can get you noticed, even if it's simply bumping into senior executives to get budgets signed off. It's a chance to shine (and potentially push ethical causes from the bottom up).

These individuals are called Social Intrapreneurs – people within a large corporation who take direct initiative for innovations that address social or environmental challenges, while also creating commercial value for the company.

If you aspire to be such a person, build the following traits and reinvent your job with purpose:

A LEARNING MINDSET
Learn as much as possible as quickly as possible and see everything you do as an opportunity to learn. Remove the stigma from mistakes and errors; they are learning opportunities.

TRUST IN YOURSELF
Have a quiet confidence that you can take on whatever may come. Instead of fearing the unknown, develop trust that you can handle whatever challenge might be next.

HUMILITY
Be open to other opinions, admit your mistakes, spend time in self-reflection and recognize that you can't do everything yourself. Accept blame and share praise. Trust others instead of micromanaging.

AND
Be resilient, be tenacious and be creative.

8. THE AGE OF THE ECO-LEADERS

Leadership is always crucial when it comes to making great changes in business, and styles of leadership have evolved over the years.

The book *Sustainable Business: A One Planet Approach* (Jeanrenaud, Jeanrenaud, Gosling) outlines this evolution to what it calls the Eco-Leader (taken originally from Simon Western's writings of 2013).

The first diagram shows the evolution of leadership styles over the last century.

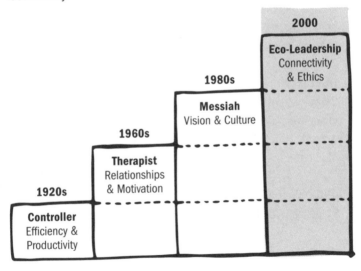

The book goes on to develop the thinking in greater detail, incorporating the four main styles and their interrelationship with ethical areas of business.

This is an interesting area to consider of oneself, or together as a leadership team.

	CONTROLLER	THERAPIST	MESSIAH	ECO-LEADERSHIP
VISION / AIMS	**Iron cage**	**Motivate to produce**	**Culture control**	**Holistic and sustainable**
	Maximizes production through transactional exchange, control and coercion.	Maximizes production through increased motivation, personal growth and teamwork.	Maximizes production through identifying with the brand's strong culture, and leader's values and mission.	Success is redefined in this new paradigm. Quality, profitability, sustainability and social responsibility are connected.

	CONTROLLER	THERAPIST	MESSIAH	ECO-LEADERSHIP
PERCEPTIONS OF EMPLOYEES	**Robots** Employees are seen as human assets.	**Clients** Employees are healed and made whole through reparation and creativity at work.	**Disciples** Employees follow the leader and aspire to be more like them.	**A Network** Employees are part of a network, with agency and with autonomy, yet also part of an interdependent, connected, greater whole.
LEADS WHAT?	**Body** Controller focuses on the body to maximize efficient production, via incentives and coercion.	**Psyche** Therapist focuses on the psyche to understand motivation, design job enrichment, and create space for self-actualizing behaviours.	**Soul** Messiah works with the soul. Followers align themselves to a vision, a cause greater than self (the company).	**Systems** Eco-leaders distribute leadership throughout the system. They make spaces for leadership to flourish.

	CONTROLLER	**THERAPIST**	**MESSIAH**	**ECO-LEADERSHIP**
ORGANIZATIONAL METAPHOR	**Machine** Takes a technical and rational view of the world, thinks in closed systems, tries to control internal environment to maximize efficiency.	**Human organism** Creates conditions for personal and team growth, linking this to organizational growth and success.	**Community** The Messiah leads a community. The emphasis is on strong cultures – the brand before the individual.	**Eco-system** Leads through connections and linking the network.
CONTROL	**Bureaucratic** Control via manipulation and strict policing.	**Humanistic** Control by emotional management and therapeutic governance.	**Culture** Policing is via self and peers. Open plan offices, lack of privacy and peer surveillance are techniques of control.	**Self-regulating systems** Control resides in the system itself. It requires resources and nurturing to self-regulate.

9. HOW TO AVOID A FIZZLE-OUT

Ethical commitment needs to run through the entire organization.

Without robust and effective internal communication, principles can easily weaken in the face of day-to-day reality, as this diagram adapted from the book *Brand Manners* (Pringle & Gordon) nicely illustrates. This is often described as a strategy/execution gap.

Board enthusiasm means little if initiatives are met with cynicism on the front line. Strategies need to be fully explained to be successfully embraced at all levels of the business.

Consider what initiatives you can undertake that will prevent high-level decisions from fizzling out further down the company.

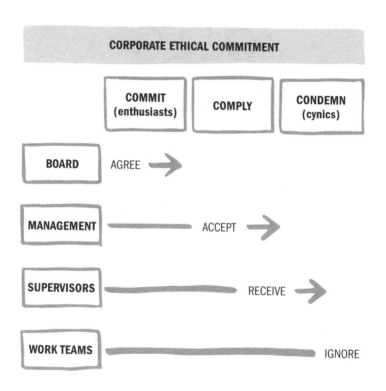

CORPORATE ETHICAL COMMITMENT

	COMMIT (enthusiasts)	COMPLY	CONDEMN (cynics)
BOARD	AGREE →		
MANAGEMENT		ACCEPT →	
SUPERVISORS			RECEIVE →
WORK TEAMS			IGNORE

10. MY EMPLOYEE ACTION PLAN

Now that you have thoroughly thought through the importance of employees, use this framework to brainstorm ideas and initiatives for greater employee engagement and happiness.

Also, consider your communications plan. And weigh up the number of initiatives in relation to your resources – see Minimum Effort, Maximum Return (Part 5.9). Resolving to do a few things well within a short time frame may be the best approach.

Try not to generate these thoughts in an ivory tower populated by senior people. Invite all levels of employees to contribute to the plan.

INITIATIVES FOR GREATER ENGAGEMENT

REMUNERATION

e.g. Living wage review

CULTURE

e.g. Creation of 'culture' team

INITIATIVES FOR GREATER ENGAGEMENT

DIVERSITY

e.g. Full diversity audit

WELLNESS

e.g. Staff food review; access to health and fitness club membership

EMPLOYEE ACTION PLAN

INITIATIVES FOR GREATER ENGAGEMENT

COMMUNITY

e.g. Company-sponsored volunteering scheme

OTHER

EMPLOYEE RECAP

1. Ask yourself why anyone should work for your company
2. Consider a more conscious culture
3. Conduct an honest diversity audit
4. Define purpose and motivation within your company
5. Examine and improve any dysfunctional teams
6. Look carefully at the way mavericks are handled and managed
7. Identify and encourage any social intrapreneurs
8. Examine styles of eco-leadership
9. Anticipate initiatives fizzling out and put appropriate measures in place
10. Create an employee action plan

ETHICAL THOUGHTS

> *"The toughest thing about the power of trust is that it's difficult to build and very easy to destroy. The essence of trust building is to emphasise the similarities between you and the customer."*
>
> Thomas J Watson

Being a trusted brand in the eyes of customers is surely the Holy Grail for any business. But trust needs to be earned.

Companies need to listen to their customers, understand what they want or need, and acknowledge them as human beings, not just consumers of product.

The ever-increasing numbers of conscious consumers are forcing companies to review their purpose – moving from selfish capitalism to responsible involvement in markets and society in general.

Businesses are nothing without customers – so ignore them at your peril and protect them well.

IN THIS PART we will turn our attention to customers and explore the importance of businesses adopting ethical stances to match consumers' concerns around environmental and ethical issues.

PART THREE

- LOYALTY
- TRUST
- COMMUNITY

HARD SELL •
THEM AND US •
EXPLOITATION •

PROTECTING
CUSTOMERS

1. THOU SHALT LOOK AFTER CUSTOMERS

Let us start with a wonderful reminder of the importance of customers with the Ten Customer Commandments list. These can be traced back to Mahatma Gandhi, who reportedly taught them to his law clerks.

1. Customers are the most important people in our business.	**6.** Customers do us a favour when they call – we do not do them a favour by serving them.
2. Customers are not dependent on us – we are dependent on them.	**7.** Customers are part of our business – they are not outsiders.
3. Customers are not to argue or match wits with.	**8.** Customers deserve the most courteous and attentive treatment we can give them.
4. Customers bring us their needs – it is our job to fulfil those needs.	**9.** Customers are the individuals who make it possible to pay our wages.
5. Customers are not an interruption of work – they are the purpose of it.	**10.** Customers are the lifeblood of this and every other business.

Source: *The Sustainable Business* (Jonathan T Scott)

Consider the following:

How do these tenets tally with your company's attitude to customers?

Which elements can you take to design your own customer charter?

What ethical stances are particularly relevant to your category or product?

2. COULD CONSCIOUS CONSUMERISM BE KILLING YOUR BUSINESS?

Conscious (or mindful) consumerism focuses on helping to balance some of the negative impacts that consumerism has on the planet.

Responsible consumerism promotes eco-friendly ways of making products, as well as creating only the amount that's needed. Other factors such as pay equality and humane working practices also drive this type of consumption.

Conscious consumers want to use their individual actions to influence global impact. At best, they will simply avoid brands that are perceived as being unethical but at worst will actively boycott them (or 'buycott', as it is now referred to). This kind of conscious consumer action is actively promoted via some apps that encourage the social sharing (and shaming) of unethical brand behaviour.

As conscious consumerism increases, those companies that fall short on ethical business criteria will lose more and more customers – ultimately killing the business if left unchecked.

So, to attract the attention of the ever-growing numbers of conscious consumers, your business needs to consider strategies that resonate with this group. We will look in greater detail over the coming sections at what specific initiatives might be right for your business, but here are some basic examples.

CUSTOMER-FACING	BEHIND THE SCENES
Pledge a percentage of profit, product or time to charity	Look after your employees
Create high-quality items in limited amounts	Connect to power from green energy suppliers
Offer some level of repairs or replacements for products (the closed loop or lake model)	Use ethical banking
	Promote sustainable production processes
Use recyclable and/or reusable materials wherever possible	Green your supply chain

3. FEED YOUR CUSTOMERS' PASSIONS

If you are an owner manager who has started a business built around a personal passion or moral crusade, you have probably grown your customer base because they buy into and share your beliefs.

If, however, you are at the stage of reviewing what your company's higher purpose can or should be, you will need to think about what's important to your customers.

These questions will help you more closely examine what your customers care deeply about and how you can potentially make a difference in that area.

What ethical issues do our customers care deeply about?

* If you cannot answer this question plainly and with authority, it suggests that you may not know your customers well enough. If this is the case, you may need to pause and commission research to ask them.

If we could do something that would make a true difference in this area, what would it be?

* The key here is in the word 'true'. Do not complete this box with platitudes. You need robust, defendable claims.

What do we need to do to deliver this?

* For example: greater knowledge; budget; manpower; innovation?

Source: *Authentic Marketing* (Larry Weber)

4. WALK IN YOUR CUSTOMERS' SHOES

Let's look at customer needs in a little more detail. To fully understand your customers, you need to get into their mindsets – with a bit of profiling. This is a highly effective general marketing exercise, but for the purpose of this book, we will focus on ethical motivations and subsequent product development responses.

First, identify your different customer types (or target audiences) and then consider the following areas/questions – putting yourself in the place of the customer:

CUSTOMER TYPE/ TARGET AUDIENCE	
ATTRIBUTES	What am I like?
MOTIVATION/ ATTITUDE	How do I view ethical and sustainability issues? What's important to me?
BRAND ASSOCIATIONS	What do I read, wear, watch, etc? What brands do I associate with?

ATTITUDINAL PHRASES	How do I express my needs?

Repeat this exercise for all your major customer types and target audiences.

Now think again about your products and services. What bits are most important to each group? How are you different from the competition? What central messaging is appropriate? And where can you reach them?

PRODUCT DEVELOPMENT	What elements of our products meet these ethical needs?
KEY DIFFERENTIATORS	What makes us so special in this area?
CUSTOMER RELATIONSHIP	What relationship do we have with this customer?
MARKETING	How can we best communicate this and in which channels?

5. TALK TO YOUR BIGGEST FANS

We often sit in boardrooms debating what our customers want and how they feel about us without actually taking the time to ask them.

These three powerful questions should be asked of your most loyal customers (but can equally be used on employees and supplier partners).

What do you love most about this company or brand?

What does this company or brand do for you that no one else does?

If this company or brand ceased to exist, what would be lost? What would you miss the most?

Source: *Conscious Capitalism Field Guide* (Sisodia, Henry, Eckschmidt)

These need to be real answers from real customers. Do not answer them internally with fanciful or 'ideal' responses that make everyone feel good.

6. IS ANYONE REALLY LISTENING?

If we are taking the time to ask customers (and other stakeholders) for input and feedback on ethical matters, it's important that we listen properly – a highly underrated skill.

The most successful people in business listen more than they speak, so that they fully understand a situation. Note: the words *listen* and *silent* share the same letters.

How good are you at listening?

Get the members of your team to fill this out privately first so that their answers are honest. Then facilitate a session in which they discuss their listening deficiencies.

Improve listening for better working effectiveness – internally and externally. If there are external listening problems, then immediately revisit the 'Talk to Your Biggest Fans' exercise.

Y/N

Dreaming
I am often thinking about something else while the other person is talking.

Answer Preparing
During conversations, I am often waiting for a pause, so I can spit out an answer that I'm already preparing.

Compulsive/Impulsive
I often say something without thinking first or to fill a silence.

Ambushing
I often fake listen just so I can get in my comments.

Judging
I practise selective listening. I hear the things I want to hear based upon my own prejudices.

Not Fully Present
I'm often unaware of the message the person is sending through body language and/or vocal intonation.

Noise-Induced Stress
I often embark on a call or meeting when there is background noise in the environment to hinder my ability to listen.

Comparing
I listen through filters, based on past experiences with other customers/colleagues.

This whole area is equally important for employees, team members, friends and family.

Here are some ways to become a better listener.

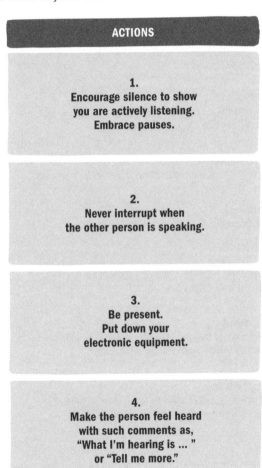

ACTIONS

1.
Encourage silence to show
you are actively listening.
Embrace pauses.

2.
Never interrupt when
the other person is speaking.

3.
Be present.
Put down your
electronic equipment.

4.
Make the person feel heard
with such comments as,
"What I'm hearing is ... "
or "Tell me more."

ACTIONS

5.
Become a solution-oriented
listener. Listen for the
intended solution
more than for problems.

6.
Listen for what is not
being said.
Find the meaning
behind the words.

7.
Resist the temptation
to rebut.
Don't argue.

Source: *The Salesperson's Secret Code* (Mills, Ridley, Laker & Chapman)

7. TIME TO PAY IT FORWARD?

We are only as good as the good we do. If a company really wants to put their money where their mouth is, considering their *nonpaying* customers in the business model will achieve this.

This may well involve giving away products or services for free.

This approach is outlined in the book *Authentic Marketing* (Larry Weber). Weber recommends asking the following big questions:

Who in the world would most benefit if they had access to our products/services?

How can we set up a programme to provide access to our products/services to those people in need?

For specific examples of this, see BOGOF Reinvented – Buy One GIVE One Free (Part 5.6).

8. ARE YOUR CUSTOMERS VAGUELY LOYAL OR FULLY COMMITTED?

Customers can appear deceptively loyal but actually be uncommitted to a brand. They might only use the brand because everyone else does or through lack of choice, affordability or simply distribution. Whichever way, the relationship can be fragile.

So basic customer satisfaction is actually a poor predictor of behaviour – commitment is much better. Loyalty is what customers *do*. Commitment is what they *feel* – a more powerful component.

Even if your customers appear fully satisfied and loyal today, as their consumer conscience rises so will their commitment to more ethical brands. A similar business with more sustainable credentials can provide an easy switch.

The evidence also shows that many customers (particularly millennials) are prepared to pay extra for more ethical and sustainable products.

What are you doing to ensure your customers are fully committed?

9. MAKE WAY FOR THE MATURING MILLENNIALS

The rise in conscious consumerism and the desire for organizations to stand for a greater moral purpose is very much being led by the younger generation. And this is an important factor for companies to acknowledge.

Businesses must avoid having the wrong people tackle these issues. Work groups must be representative of all relevant factions and, specifically, recognize the importance of millennials.

Always bear in mind that this is the audience that has the greatest sway in most markets and votes with its feet on ethical issues.

AS CUSTOMERS	AS EMPLOYEES
68% of US millennials want to be known for making a positive difference in the world.	88% of millennials say their job is more fulfilling when they're provided with opportunities to make a positive impact on social and environmental issues.
81% of US millennials said a successful business needs to have a genuine purpose that resonates with people.	78% of US millennials want the values of their employer to match their own.
81% of millennials expect companies to declare their corporate citizenship publicly.	76% of millennials consider a company's social and environmental commitments when deciding where to work.
	75% of millennials would take a pay cut to work for a socially responsible company.
73% of US millennials are willing to pay extra for sustainable offerings.	64% of millennials won't take a job if a potential employer doesn't have strong CSR practices.
	75% of US millennials define success as doing work that has a positive impact on society.

Sources: *WEconomy* (Kielburger, Branson & Kielburger), *Huffington Post, Cone Comms CSR Study 2016, American Express, Forbes*

10. MY CUSTOMER ACTION PLAN

Now that you have thoroughly thought through the significance of your customers, use this framework to brainstorm ideas and initiatives for greater customer engagement and satisfaction.

At this point, also consider your other stakeholder groups (as identified in Part 1). For example, your supplier network. What initiatives would help forge greater relationships with your suppliers?

INITIATIVES FOR GREATER ENGAGEMENT

CUSTOMER SATISFACTION

e.g. Customer 'thank you' programme

FEEDING PASSIONS

e.g. Regional focus groups (qualitative research); e-mail questionnaire (quantitative research)

INITIATIVES FOR GREATER ENGAGEMENT

PAYING IT FORWARD

e.g. New BOGOF initiative (see Part 5.6)

SUPPLIER RELATIONS

e.g. Supplier 'charter'

COMMUNITY

e.g. Local community events calendar

OTHER

CUSTOMER RECAP

1. Consider the Ten Customer Commandments and draw up your own version
2. Look at the rise in conscious consumerism and identify specific trends in your market
3. Identify the ethical issues your customers care about and then feed their passion
4. Walk in your customers' shoes by examining their views and matching your products and services to them
5. Identify your major fans and actually talk to them
6. Encourage active listening internally among your teams and externally with customers and stakeholders
7. Consider who in the world could benefit from your product and how you can potentially Pay it Forward
8. Look at the distinction between apparent customer loyalty and commitment
9. Examine and quantify the large market of maturing millennials to see what impact they have on your business
10. Create a customer action plan

ETHICAL THOUGHTS

"Right now, we are facing a man-made disaster of global scale. Our greatest threat in thousands of years. Climate change. If we don't take action, the collapse of our civilizations and the extinction of much of the natural world is on the horizon."

David Attenborough

Being environmentally friendly used to be regarded as a nicety in business – somewhat fluffy, something to appease environmental pressure groups, and probably rather costly and inconvenient.

This is no longer the case. The evidence now shows that reducing negative impact on the planet is a vital prerequisite of running a successful business. Customers demand ethical practices, and they actively 'buycott' companies that do not demonstrate them.

The definition of sustainability is that something sustains. So in essence, companies that do not protect the planet's resources will not endure.

Transforming into a sustainable, environmentally conscious business can seem very daunting, but it is important to look at the simple steps that can be taken first. You'll never achieve everything at once.

Instead of being paralyzed by the sheer scale of the challenge, head toward the easiest paths. If every company could simply start making the changes they can, the planet would be in a much healthier place.

IN THIS PART we will take a more detailed look at the range of actions businesses can take to protect the planet's resources.

PART FOUR

- SUSTAINABILITY
- RECYCLING
- CONSERVATION

GREED •
OVER-CONSUMPTION •
THOUGHTLESSNESS •

PROTECTING THE PLANET

1. THERE IS NO PLANET B

"There is no planet B. We have to take care of the one we have."
Richard Branson

And he's right. When it comes to the damage people, businesses and governments are doing to the planet, there is no plan B once our resources are destroyed.

So it must be down to each of us to do what we can to protect the environment in which we live.

For businesses, the primary question is:

Are we taking more from the planet than we are putting back?

If the answer is yes, then start to consider some of these remedial areas:

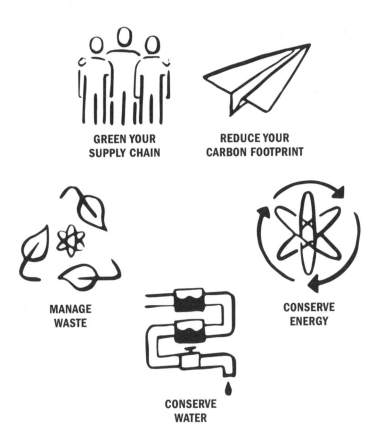

GREEN YOUR SUPPLY CHAIN

REDUCE YOUR CARBON FOOTPRINT

MANAGE WASTE

CONSERVE WATER

CONSERVE ENERGY

And remember, you cannot manage what you don't measure. Initiatives in all these areas require clear metrics for monitoring and reporting.

One way that companies can quantify their environmental impact is by understanding the concept of *Natural Capital*.

Natural capital is not produced by mankind – nature gives it to us for free. Non-renewables such as oil and gas can only be used once, whereas renewables such as air, water and fish stocks will continue, so long as we do not over pollute or drive a species to extinction.

Together, they are the foundation that ensures our survival and wellbeing, and the basis of all economic activity. It is possible to account for, measure and value these resources, and generate sustainable growth by sticking to one rule: *the aggregate level of natural capital should not decline.* The father of this concept is Dieter Helm; for a full picture of this issue read his book, *Natural Capital*.

2. REDUCING YOUR CARBON FOOTPRINT

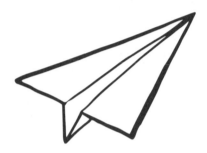

A carbon footprint is the amount of carbon dioxide released into the atmosphere as a result of the activities of a particular individual, organization or community.

Carbon dioxide absorbs and traps heat. The more carbon dioxide in the atmosphere, the warmer the planet.

There is now very clear evidence that this man-made climate change is causing catastrophic harm to our planet.

This is a complex and highly debated subject, and we will try to break it down further in the next few pages, but on the next page there's a simple overview of how to start on a journey toward carbon neutrality in your business.

Step 1. **UNDERSTAND YOUR** **EMISSIONS**	• Utilities • Fuel • Production • Travel • Paper • Shipping • Packaging
Step 2. **REDUCE DIRECT** **EMISSIONS**	• Energy use • Supply chain • Infrastructure
Step 3. **OFFSET THE BALANCE** **OF WHAT YOU** **CANNOT REDUCE**	• With high quality carbon credits
	= NET ZERO EMISSIONS

This is great, but scientists generally agree that carbon neutrality won't necessarily be enough to address climate change. Neutrality is clearly very important but it's not the end goal.

Interface is an example of a company taking this further with their Climate Take Back mission. This invites industry to commit to running businesses in a way that is restorative to the planet, to use products and services to reverse the effects of global warming, and to create a climate fit for life.

For more details, visit: *www.interface.com*

3. CONSERVING ENERGY

The first step here is straightforward – switch to a renewable energy supplier.

But there are many other ways you can reduce how much energy you use and lower costs in the workplace.

SMART METERING

Installing smart meters can have the greatest overall effect on managing energy in the workplace and at home. Smart meters come with a display screen that shows the user exactly how much energy they're using and what it costs, in near real time.

TIME-OF-USE TARIFFS

Time-of-use tariffs are designed to incentivize customers to use more electricity at off-peak times in order to balance demand. These tariffs charge cheaper rates at certain times of the night or day, when demand is at its lowest, and higher rates at popular times. Shifting demand to off-peak times means relying less on polluting sources of electricity.

TRAVEL

Travel is another important factor. Can meeting technology reduce the need for physical business travel? If travel is essential, should a company commit to a carbon-offsetting programme? Are employees encouraged to cycle to work, use public transport or work from home whenever possible?

GENERAL

A good source for recommendations, downloadable guides and case histories to help businesses reduce their environmental impact is *CarbonTrust.com*. Their suggestions include:

- **SWITCH OFF**
  Switch off all non-essential lighting out of business hours. Most people say this is so obvious but think of all the buildings you still see lit up at night.

- **PHOTOCELL CONTROLS**
  Install photocell controls to switch off some lighting on brighter days.

- **LED FITTINGS**
  Replace traditional tungsten lamps with energy-efficient LED fittings to improve efficiency and reduce operating costs.

- **TIMING**
  Experiment with switch-on and switch-off times for heating and air conditioning and switch off before the end of the working day.

- **THERMOSTATS**
  Ensure thermostats are set correctly – increase temperature set-points for cooling and reduce set-points for heating.

- **TURN OFF**

  Turn off unnecessary equipment during the day and especially after hours to reduce heat build-up and unnecessary electrical costs.

- **INSULATION**

  Check insulation levels and increase wherever practical to reduce heating requirements.

- **MONITOR**

  Walk around your office at different times of the day and during different seasons to see how and when heaters and coolers are working. Check time and temperature settings.

Positive change does not happen if this sits somewhere on a policy sheet. Intentions need to be converted into clear, specific action points for individuals to carry out.

4. CONSERVING WATER

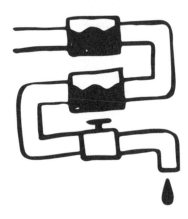

Each person, on average, uses 150 litres of water per day. If everyone in the UK adopted more water-saving habits, this could easily be reduced to 100 litres per day.

Businesses can play a big part. Here are some tips:

- **LOOK OUT FOR WATER LEAKS**
  We lose three billion litres of water a day in England and Wales due to water leaks.

- **INSTALL DUAL-FLUSH TOILETS**
  Toilets represent over 30% of water usage in the workplace. If your building is open to the public, this can be even more substantial. Dual flush toilets use six litres on full flush, which is less than half of a traditional toilet.

- **INSTALL EFFICIENT TAPS**
  Make sure all your hand basin taps are on auto shut-off. Also, you can buy aerators – these spread the stream of water coming out of your tap into tiny droplets. This will prevent splashing and save water.

- **FILL THE DISHWASHER**
  Always wash a full load of dishes to gain maximum water efficiency. If possible, change to a water-efficient dishwasher, as it uses the minimal amount of water necessary to clean and rinse.

- **ENCOURAGE SHORT SHOWERS**
  If your workplace has showers, spread the word that spending over five minutes in a Power Shower can use more water than taking a bath.

- **DON'T WASTE DRINKING WATER**
  The Department of Health recommends that we drink at least one litre of water each day (about six glasses). Many people waste water by letting the tap run cold before filling up their glass. So keep jugs of water in the fridge or install a water fountain that serves ice-cold drinking water straight away.

5. NOT ALL WASTE IS BORN EQUAL

The headlines here are:
1. REDUCE the amount you use
2. REUSE product or product elements, wherever possible
3. RECYCLE what is left, wherever possible

The Waste Hierarchy model sets out the levels of options for managing waste in an environmentally helpful way.

It gives top priority to preventing waste in the first place. When waste *is* created, it gives priority to preparing it for reuse, then recycling, then recovery, and last of all disposal (e.g. landfill) – which should be avoided whenever possible.

STAGES	INCLUDE

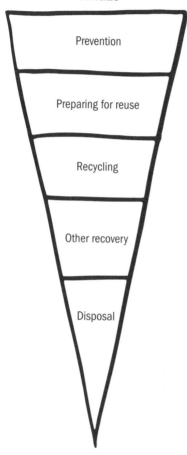

STAGES

Prevention

Preparing for reuse

Recycling

Other recovery

Disposal

INCLUDE

Using less material in design and manufacture. Keeping products for longer. Reuse.

Checking, cleaning, repairing, refurbishing, whole items or spare parts.

Turning waste into a new substance or product (including composting).

Includes anaerobic digestion, incineration with energy recovery, gasification and pyrolysis which produce energy (fuels, heat and power) and materials from waste.

Landfill and incineration without energy recovery.

Source: *Defra.gov.uk – the official website for the Department for Environment, Food and Rural Affairs*

6. IS YOUR BUSINESS A RIVER OR LAKE?

Another way to look at waste management is with the river versus lake analogy described below.

Current business production systems tend to operate on a linear (or river) model, where materials are used to make products, which are then consumed and disposed of. And this is the last that we see of them.

Sustainable business practice promotes a circular (or lake) model – meaning wherever possible resources are recaptured and brought back into productive use. This minimizes waste and ensures less 'virgin' material is needed at source. This can be done through refurbishing, repairing, reusing, remanufacturing and recycling.

Consider these two models and how you can adopt a more circular approach to your business and throughout your supply chain.

RIVER MODEL

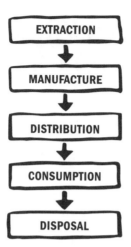

EXTRACTION
↓
MANUFACTURE
↓
DISTRIBUTION
↓
CONSUMPTION
↓
DISPOSAL

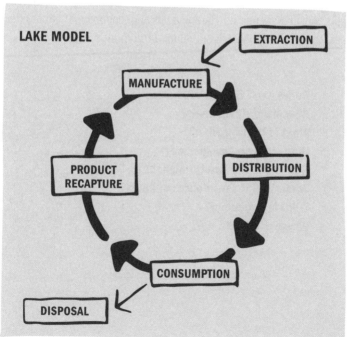

LAKE MODEL

EXTRACTION

MANUFACTURE

DISTRIBUTION

PRODUCT RECAPTURE

CONSUMPTION

DISPOSAL

7. GREENING YOUR SUPPLY CHAIN

All businesses rely on a chain of suppliers – whether for products or services.

PRODUCTS

We have looked at how to reduce our corporate carbon footprint and conserve resources. Here is a set of questions that should be asked of your supply chain in relation to product:

- **Do we need this (at all)?**
- **Who made it? And how?**
- **What is it wrapped in?**
- **How will it be transported?**
- **How will it perform throughout its life?**
- **What does it say to our customers?**
- **What is it made of?**
- **Where will it end up?**

Source: *WEconomy* (Kielburger, Branson, Kielburger)

AN ADDITIONAL NOTE ON PACKAGING

Packaging comes in many shapes and sizes: boxes, bags, cans, foam pellets, shrink wrap, tubes, paper, etc. – all designed to protect a product and keep it pristine or fresh.

When considering packaging in your supply chain, make sure you cover the various types:

- **Primary packaging**: the wrapping or container handled by customers
- **Secondary packaging**: larger cases, boxes or bags used to group goods together for distribution, ease of carrying or displaying in shops
- **Transit packaging**: pallets, boards, plastic wrap and containers used to collate products into larger loads for shipping

SERVICES

Supply chains also include service providers. These should also be added to your assessment.

Are they committed to renewable energy?

What environmental policies do they have?

Will you refuse to work with companies unless they can meet your expectations on ethical and sustainable behaviour?

And a final note on the UK Modern Slavery Act, which came into effect in 2015. This requires companies to make a public statement on whether they have processes in place to look into modern slavery anywhere in their operations or their supply chain. Technically only multimillion-pound turnover companies need to publish a statement on this (on the main page of their website), but it's an area that all companies should consider.

8. ARE YOU AN ECO- OR EGO-WARRIOR?

Are you an Eco-Warrior – genuinely concerned with the planet and civilization as a whole? Or are you an Ego-Warrior – more focused on how your actions are viewed by your peers?

While clearly the latter has a degree of cynicism attached, the truth is that as long as you are adapting your behaviour to help protect the planet, the result is still positive.

The same can be said of business. Notwithstanding the importance of marketing authenticity (covered in Part 5), the motivation to create a more ethical and sustainable business can vary. For example:

- Some will be driven by a personal eco crusade
- For others, the positive PR will be an attractive factor (and fuel the corporate ego)
- Arguing the positive effect on the bottom line will delight the finance department
- HR will be keen to capitalize on attracting and retaining better talent
- Customer service will welcome a happy, committed customer base

Your customers will also have different motivations and reasons for selecting more ethical and sustainable products. For some it will be a genuine commitment to saving the planet. For others it will be a trade off to feel better about consumption in other areas. Ultimately, the planet doesn't care much about motive, just action.

So the moral here is that whatever pushes the ethical agenda along in your business is positive progress.

9. OVERCOMING THE RESISTORS

There will always be some resistance to adopting ethical and sustainable practices. Here are some of the common ones.

Consider the issues and think of ways to overcome them.

ISSUE	TYPICAL RESPONSE	WAYS TO OVERCOME
LACK OF AWARENESS Ignorance is the greatest enemy of sustainability.	"I didn't know it was a big issue."	Show the compelling facts and stats.
DEFEATISM An acceptance that this is just part of business.	"It's not worth all the effort."	Show long-term benefits. Explain the downside if not done.
THE COST MYTH Ignoring the savings and potential profits.	"How much is this going to cost?"	Explain cost-saving benefits.
THE HASSLE FACTOR Not considering it part of job description.	"I've got enough on my plate."	Lobby for more resources. Make it part of everyone's job description.

ISSUE	TYPICAL RESPONSE	WAYS TO OVERCOME
SCEPTICISM It's impossible to prove.	"Let's wait and see ..."	Show competitor actions, plus the compelling facts and stats.
SOCIAL LOAFING Happy to leave it to the eco-warriors.	"Someone else can do it."	Incentivize for joining in. Have sanctions for not getting involved.
TOO SIMPLE Solutions feel too simple and low-tech to take seriously.	"Turn the lights off? Everyone knows that."	Show the cumulative stats – small actions making big differences.

Source: adapted from *The Sustainable Business* (Jonathan T Scott)

10. MY PLANET ACTION PLAN

Now that you have considered all the ways you and your company can help protect the planet, use the following framework to brainstorm specific ideas and initiatives.

INITIATIVES FOR ENVIRONMENTAL SUSTAINABILITY

REDUCING CARBON FOOTPRINT

e.g. Staff canteen review (local suppliers, increased vegetarian options); business travel review

CONSERVING ENERGY

e.g. Switch to renewable energy supplier; create an internal 'Green Team'

PLANET ACTION PLAN

INITIATIVES FOR ENVIRONMENTAL SUSTAINABILITY

CONSERVING WATER

e.g. Upgrade staff/ customer toilet facilities; invest in high-quality artificial plants

MANAGING WASTE

e.g. Create Reduce, Reuse, Recycle programme; conduct single-use plastics review

INITIATIVES FOR ENVIRONMENTAL SUSTAINABILITY

GREENING SUPPLY CHAIN

e.g. Create 'Green Supplier Charter'; review all packaging (primary, secondary, transit)

OTHER

PLANET RECAP

1. Work out whether you are taking more from the planet than you are putting back
2. Identify areas where you can reduce your carbon footprint
3. Create an energy conservation plan
4. Create a water conservation plan
5. Create a waste management plan
6. Consider whether you can move the business from a river model to a lake model
7. Create a plan to green your supply chain
8. Contrast ego- with eco-warriors and harness their joint power
9. Anticipate areas of resistance to progressing as an ethical and sustainable business and develop plans to overcome them
10. Now create a planet action plan

ETHICAL THOUGHTS

> *"People who say it cannot be done should not interrupt those who are doing it."*
>
> George Bernard Shaw

Assuming a company is indeed behaving ethically, its marketing will immediately gain extra credence and authenticity.

Rather than scrabbling around for the standard calendar-based marketing clichés (Valentine's, Easter, Halloween, Christmas, etc.), businesses can instead focus on the genuinely interesting initiatives they are enacting.

In short, the marketing efforts of an ethical business are essentially self-defining, unforced and, therefore, genuinely engaging.

But don't be afraid of the halfway house – all businesses are a work in progress. Companies just need to be able to legitimately say that initiatives have been set in train and that this is part of an ethical journey to better things. Just be sure that any claims do not fall into the category of greenwashing. You will be exposed for false marketing, and this can do far more harm than good.

Stick to the truth, be honest and update stakeholders regularly on your progress.

IN THIS PART we will further explore the benefits and pitfalls of placing ethical beliefs and activities at the heart of your marketing and communications strategy.

PART FIVE

- ENGAGING
- AUTHENTIC
- HUMAN

GREENWASHING •
DISINGENUOUS •
MISLEADING •

ETHICAL MARKETING

1. MARKETING – FROM MANIPULATION TO AUTHENTICITY

Marketing has come a long way. Here's a nice reminder of its evolution and thoughts on the new age of authentic marketing practices.

The moral of this evolution is that modern companies must pay attention to their customers and evolve. Failure to do so will severely jeopardize customer trust – a crucial element in marketing today.

PRODUCTION ERA 1860s to 1920s	During this time, companies pushed products at people – believing that if they developed a quality product, it would sell. Businesses focused primarily on manufacturing.
SALES ERA 1920s to 1940s	During the Great Depression, people bought only the necessities and supply often exceeded demand. Competition was more intense. This drove companies to turn up the volume on the hard sell, heavily using advertising to push their products at people.

MARKETING ERA Mid-20th century	Here came a fundamental shift in focus: from the needs of the seller to the needs of the buyer. Broadcast advertising emerged, giving companies new ways to capture attention – to interrupt and manipulate. However, it was now done creatively – with likeable characters, celebrity endorsements, etc.
RELATIONSHIP MARKETING ERA Mid-1990s to early 2000s	Recognizing that acquiring new customers was more expensive than keeping current ones, marketing folk began to value the role of relationships and brand loyalty. Big data emerged as a means to help companies better understand audience segmentation. Direct marketing became a staple tactic.
DIGITAL ENGAGEMENT ERA 2000s	As the internet and digital/social media started to become engrained in our culture, a seismic shift happened. A massive power shift put the reins directly in the hands of consumers, who now had the strongest and most important voice in the conversation. Engagement was the word.
AUTHENTIC MARKETING ERA 2018-	To thrive and truly engage in today's elaborate environment, we need to continue to push marketing to its most evolved form yet – one of authenticity. The missing critical piece – moral purpose – holds the potential to propel companies by adding the values and ethical impact customers crave and demand.

Source: *Authentic Marketing* (Larry Weber).

2. THE NEW PRINCIPLES OF ETHICAL MARKETING

To adopt a new ethical approach to marketing, you will need to challenge some of your existing habits and behaviours.

Gather your team and generate an honest assessment of where your company or brand sits in each of the following categories.

If everything falls to the right of the chart, then you can stop reading this book ...

	CONVENTIONAL MARKETING	**ETHICAL MARKETING**
CONSUMERS	Consumers with lifestyles	People with lives
PRODUCTS	Cradle-to-grave products Globally sourced One size fits all	Cradle-to-cradle services (G)locally sourced Regionally tailored
MARKETING AND COMMUNICATIONS	Product end-benefits Paid advertising Selling One-way communication	Purpose Word-of-mouth Educating and empowering Creating community
CORPORATE	Secretive Reactive Independent and autonomous Competitive	Transparent Proactive Interdependent/allied with stakeholders Cooperative

Source: adapted from *The New Rules of Green Marketing* (Jacquelyn Ottman)

3. GREENWASHING WON'T WASH

> **WHITEWASH** (verb): *to make something bad seem acceptable by hiding the truth.*
>
> **GREENWASH** (verb): *to make people believe that your company is doing more to protect the environment than it really is.*

As we have said before, you don't have to be perfect, but you absolutely need to be honest when you consider promoting your ethical credentials. False marketing claims will be exposed, and that all-important trust will be lost overnight.

GREENWASHING IS RIFE:

- 26% of companies have no proof to back up their claims
- 11% of labelling is vague
- 4% of green claims are irrelevant
- 1% even make claims to distract customers from deficiencies (such as 'organically grown tobacco')
- 1% are out-and-out lies

Source: *The Sustainable Business* (Jonathan T Scott)

Ethical marketing requires complete transparency. Be proud of your positive actions but also acknowledge and be honest about the areas that you need to work on. Then tell customers what you plan to do about it and when. Don't be afraid of outlining why it's not an easy, quick fix.

If there are suspicions over claims in your marketing, consider commissioning an independent source to audit and verify your claims. You may be surprised at the result.

4. TOO LITTLE, TOO TRIUMPHANT, TOO LATE?

It's not just greenwashing you have to watch out for. Many companies come unstuck in their marketing when they fail to understand the bigger picture.

This usually falls into the following categories: too little, too triumphant, too late.

So consider the following.

IS IT TOO LITTLE?

- Is this claim too insignificant in the grand scale of things?
- Do we run the risk of being ridiculed for this?
- Will this simply highlight bigger areas of the business that are currently unethical?

Example: Companies proudly reporting that they have removed plastic straws from the business, while simultaneously ignoring all other single use plastics being used throughout the organization.

IS IT TOO TRIUMPHANT?

- Is this an isolated claim that we are making an overly big fuss about?
- Could this solicit negative customer feedback because it feels somewhat incongruent in relation to other unethical parts of the business?

Example: Companies making a huge song and dance about one ethical activity such as charity giving, while continuing to adopt unethical and unsustainable practices elsewhere in the organization.

IS IT TOO LATE?

- Have all our competitors been doing this for ages?
- Does this simply highlight how late to the party we are?

Example: Companies reporting to care deeply about customers' data and requesting that they re-subscribe for special and unique offers and promotions, in the very month that GDPR (General Data Protection Regulation) becomes a legal requirement.

Be honest with this assessment and ruthlessly analyse possible marketing claims from a purely marketing perspective. They may be true, but will they be positively received?

5. STORYDOING AND DATATELLING

Bringing out the human side of your brand can help forge stronger and deeper connections with customers. The book *Authentic Marketing* (Larry Weber) looks at specific engagement efforts that can make your brand more human and your marketing more authentic.

First, consider the following in terms of your brand.

PUT HONESTY FIRST	Communicating openly and honestly is crucial in today's untrusting world.
STAND OUT BY STANDING UP	Companies today are expected to take a stand on issues and demonstrate they are working to solve societal problems.

BE PROACTIVE	Be bold, be proactive and stand out in your marketplace with messages that catch people's attention.
PAINT THE FACES OF YOUR BRAND	Putting some of the faces in your company front and centre is a powerful way to reveal the human side of your organization.
SAY YOU'RE SORRY	Humanizing your brand also means owning up to problems. and apologizing – fast!
DITCH THE CORPORATE SPEAK	Customers don't trust corporate-speak. They don't relate to it, and they tune out as soon as they hear it.
SHOW YOUR FUNNY BONE	Don't be afraid to show your lighter side. Making people laugh is an engaging way to bring forth the human side of your brand.

Authentic Marketing also talks of storydoing and datatelling. As the author says, this may sound like marketing speak, but it's really about moving your organization from telling stories to actually being an active part of them. This is all about showing what your company is *doing* to solve a problem to make the world a better place.

It is also important to outline measurable objectives that your company can realistically accomplish in a certain time period – then track and measure them as you make progress. Quantifiable data is important to validate this progress and should be included in the narrative. It can be used to create simple/powerful visuals, charts, graphs and marketing claims.

Here are some techniques for creating compelling, ongoing stories that bring your moral purpose to life.

TELL IT VISUALLY	Without a doubt, visual is the best format today. Repurpose stories across multiple visual media for maximum impact.
BE SELECTIVE WITH WORDS	Use words that are vibrant, descriptive, evoke emotions, ignite the senses and draw readers in.
ENSURE IT'S ALWAYS ON	Your company's ethical journey will have a beginning and many chapters but should not have an end. It should be living, breathing and evolving.
HIGHLIGHT HUMILITY	Bring forth the people in your stories. Share their voices (including employees, customers and suppliers).
LET CREATIVITY SHINE	Make the best use of the technical tools now readily available and tell stories with creativity.
KEEP IT REAL	People will sniff out even the slightest hint of manipulation or marketing speak – so keep it honest and genuine, with a little dose of humility (and no hubris).

6. BOGOF REINVENTED –
BUY ONE, GIVE ONE FREE

One of the most impactful and tangible strategies a company can consider builds on the paying it forward approach (Part 3.7).

Once you have identified people who would benefit most from your product or service but are unable to afford it, you can develop a plan to incorporate an element of free distribution as part of your triple bottom line business plan.

For the ultimate in clear, powerful marketing messages, you can reinvent the old promotional tool of Buy One Get One Free to **Buy One GIVE One Free.**

This is now being successfully used by a number of innovative, thoughtful businesses:

TOMS SHOES
Toms Shoes improves lives through a programme they call One for One. For every product purchased they provide shoes, sight, water, safe birth and bullying prevention services to people in need.

MINDFUL CHEF

Mindful Chef, a healthy food recipe and delivery service, runs a programme called One Feeds Two. With every meal purchased, they donate a school meal to a child in poverty, which has amounted to over one million so far.

HEY GIRLS

Hey Girls tackles period poverty in the UK by giving a free box of sanitary towels to women and girls in need for every box purchased. This buy one give one approach gives girls the freedom to enjoy normal lives without having to miss school, ask friends for products or simply go without.

Not all organizations can commit to the full buy one, give one model. If this doesn't work for your business, consider instead a **Buy One, Give SOMETHING** approach.

Another initiative that you may already be aware of is Pledge 1% – pioneered by SalesForce.org. Here companies pledge to annually give 1% of equity, 1% of profits, 1% of product and/or 1% of employee time to worthy causes.

So consider to whom you could give your product (time and/or profit) and how it could become part of your marketing story.

7. NAVIGATING THE COMPETITION

The market mapping tool is a highly effective and very flexible way to establish clarity and strategic authority when looking at any market.

In this instance, it can be used to monitor your ethical progress and integrity against your competition. This is a fast-moving area, so this exercise needs to be done regularly to ensure your ethical authority is justified – to check that your competitors are not outdoing your achievements and therefore rendering your marketing claims weak or untrue.

For this 'ethical' exercise, we will use a vertical axis on Profitability against a horizontal axis of Ethical Credentials. Place your company plus your competitors on the grid. Use the results to identify where you currently sit within your marketplace against where you would like to be.

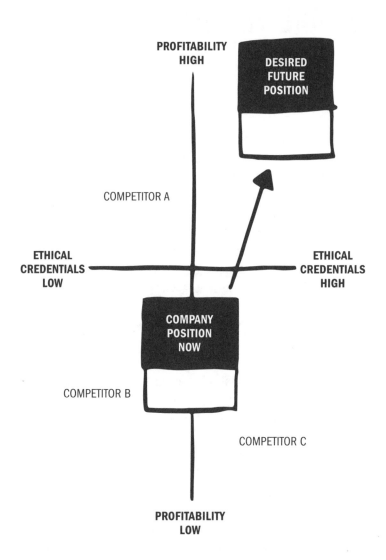

8. ARE YOU AN ETHICAL GAME CHANGER?

The Three Buckets exercise was introduced by Adam Morgan in his book *The Pirate Inside*. It is an extremely helpful way to categorize ideas or projects and work out how effective they are likely to be and also how genuinely 'unique' they are.

In the case of ethical marketing initiatives, it's important that you have the right mix. If they are all fairly basic, you will struggle to stand out against your competitors. If they are all overly innovative, you run the risk of being seen as ignoring the obvious.

The exercise is to place ideas and initiatives in one of the three buckets.

On the left is **Brilliant Basics**. These represent 'excellence as standard'. You or your company should really be doing these well as a matter of course, just like your competitors.

In the middle is **Compelling Difference**. These should be 'significantly better than normal'. These are demonstrably better than your competitors, but not genuinely remarkable.

On the right is **Changing the Game**. These are 'truly extraordinary'. They are utterly distinctive in the market and genuinely remarkable.

BRILLIANT BASICS	COMPELLING DIFFERENCE	CHANGING THE GAME

Ideally, everything on the left should be underway or completed.
If there is nothing in the middle or right, you need better initiatives.

9. MINIMUM EFFORT, MAXIMUM RETURN

Once you have your comprehensive list of ethical and sustainable initiatives, it's important to prioritize these and balance business impact with the effort or resources required. It is better to complete a few really important initiatives than to start many and finish few.

Here's a neat framework adapted from the book *Conscious Capitalism Field Guide* (Sisodia, Henry, Eckschmidt), which allows you to compare the estimated resources required (effort) against the impact on the business – whether that's customer excitement, employee engagement, environmental protection or financial reward (return).

Resources are relative to the size of your organization. What might take three or four people would be a high resource in a start-up, but easy for a large organization.

Using this matrix will help you identify four types of initiative:

TOP LEFT: High return, low effort initiatives = do them now
TOP RIGHT: High return, high effort initiatives = plan them now
BOTTOM LEFT: Low effort, low return initiatives = consider further
BOTTOM RIGHT: High effort, low return initiatives = ignore

Gather your team together and spend as long as the business requires filling in the matrix. Then draw up an action plan based on the outcome.

HIGH RETURN, LOW EFFORT	**HIGH RETURN HIGH EFFORT**
DO NOW	PLAN
THINK ON	IGNORE
LOW EFFORT, LOW RETURN	**HIGH EFFORT, LOW RETURN**

Another useful matrix, from *Business Ethics – Oxford University Press* (Crane & Matten), allows you to plot initiatives based on cost versus feel-good factors.

TOP LEFT: Low cost, high feel-good factor = do now

TOP RIGHT: High cost, high feel-good factor = plan and budget now

BOTTOM LEFT: Low cost, low feel-good factor = consider further

TOP LEFT: High cost, low feel-good factor = ignore

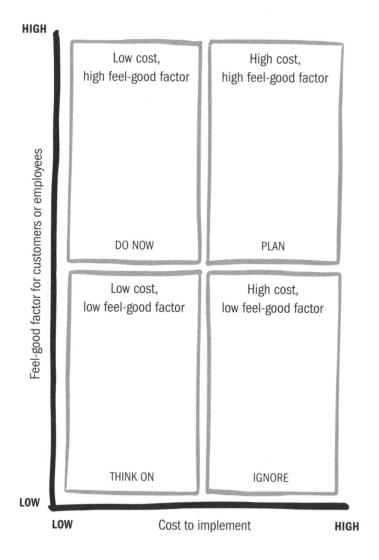

10. THE INFINITE ETHICAL LOOP

Becoming a more ethical and sustainable business is not a one-off project – it requires constant review to even try to stay on top of the game. We learn more about human behaviour and the state of our planet every day, so this should be viewed as an ever-evolving landscape.

Although the bulk of thinking around your moral purpose will be done at the outset, the impact of the resulting initiatives needs to be closely monitored and the data reviewed so that you can successfully continue to protect profits, people and the planet.

So keep going around the loop.

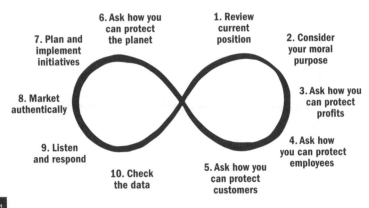

6. Ask how you can protect the planet

1. Review current position

7. Plan and implement initiatives

2. Consider your moral purpose

8. Market authentically

3. Ask how you can protect profits

9. Listen and respond

4. Ask how you can protect employees

10. Check the data

5. Ask how you can protect customers

1. **Review current position**

2. **Consider your moral purpose**

3. **Ask how you can protect profits**

4. **Ask how you can protect employees**

5. **Ask how you can protect customers**

6. **Ask how you can protect the planet**

7. **Plan and implement initiatives**

8. **Market authentically**

9. **Listen and respond**

10. **Check the data**

MARKETING RECAP

1. Understand the characteristics of the authentic marketing era
2. Examine the new principles of ethical marketing
3. Audit and remove any examples of greenwashing
4. Screen all marketing claims that may be too little, too late, or too triumphant
5. Look at storydoing and datatelling by using actions, facts and measurement as the basis for marketing claims
6. Work out who you could give your product to for free, and how it would fit into your marketing story
7. Keep track of your claims in relation to those of your competition and how they are changing
8. Conduct a three buckets exercise
9. Complete the minimal effort, maximum return grids
10. Use the infinite ethical loop to keep the process alive and ongoing

ETHICAL THOUGHTS

FINAL WORD

When I embarked on this book, one of my main objectives was to highlight to companies the need to make actual change for the good of people and the planet – not just expect the marketing department to come up with engaging and compelling campaigns and content with little or no substance behind them.

What I have learned is that the challenge is greater than I had appreciated. It is not easy for companies to retrospectively refit their business in a perfectly ethical way. But organizations can make significant strides in the right direction if they really want to, and genuinely buy in to the benefits associated with being more ethical and sustainable. The good ones are being proactive now, not simply waiting to react to growing public opinion.

The more I read, the more I am convinced that customers have had enough of greedy corporations exploiting the planet's resources. They are demanding better, and they are voting with their feet.

There will continue to be climate change deniers, and there are, without doubt, challenges at a higher international level that are outside of our control. But the good news is that the subject is now firmly on the agenda.

In September 2015, the UN's General Assembly adopted the 2030 Agenda for Sustainable Development.

So I'd like to conclude with a look at the bigger picture – these 17 Sustainable Development Goals (SDGs) designed to *transform our world* and promote prosperity while protecting the planet:

GOAL 1:
NO POVERTY
End poverty in all its forms – everywhere.

GOAL 2:
ZERO HUNGER
End hunger, achieve food security and improved nutrition, and promote sustainable agriculture.

GOAL 3:
GOOD HEALTH AND WELLBEING
Ensure healthy lives and promote wellbeing for all, at all ages.

GOAL 4:
QUALITY EDUCATION
Ensure inclusive and equitable
quality education and promote lifelong
learning opportunities for all.

GOAL 5:
GENDER EQUALITY
Achieve gender equality and
empower all women and girls.

GOAL 6:
CLEAN WATER AND SANITATION
Ensure availability and sustainable
management of water and sanitation for all.

GOAL 7:
AFFORDABLE AND CLEAN ENERGY
Ensure access to affordable, reliable,
sustainable and modern energy for all.

GOAL 8:
DECENT WORK AND ECONOMIC GROWTH
Promote sustained, inclusive and sustainable
economic growth, full and productive
employment, and decent work for all.

GOAL 9:
INDUSTRY, INNOVATION
AND INFRASTRUCTURE
Build resilient infrastructure, promote
inclusive and sustainable industrialization,
and foster innovation.

GOAL 10:
REDUCED INEQUALITIES
Reduce inequalities within and
among countries.

GOAL 11:
SUSTAINABLE CITIES
AND COMMUNITIES
Make cities and human settlements
inclusive, safe, resilient and sustainable.

GOAL 12:
RESPONSIBLE CONSUMPTION
AND PRODUCTION
Ensure sustainable consumption
and production patterns.

GOAL 13:
CLIMATE ACTION
Take urgent action to combat
climate change.

GOAL 14:
LIFE BELOW WATER
Conserve and sustainably use the oceans,
seas and marine resources.

GOAL 15:
LIFE ON LAND
Protect, restore and promote sustainable
use of terrestrial ecosystems, sustainably
manage forests, combat desertification, and
halt land degradation and biodiversity loss.

GOAL 16:
PEACE, JUSTICE AND
STRONG INSTITUTIONS
Promote peaceful and inclusive societies
for sustainable development and
provide access to justice for all.

GOAL 17:
PARTNERSHIPS FOR THE GOALS
Strengthen the means of implementation,
and revitalise global partnerships for
sustainable development.

For more details, visit: *www.un.org/sustainabledevelopment*

These are indeed lofty goals, but they address the global challenges we now face.

We all have a responsibility for protecting the people around us, and our planet. Researching this book has affected my own behaviour (in business and at home). But I also know I have a long way to go.

So I hope you will join me in making the changes (big or small) that you can and, fingers crossed, collectively we can make a difference.

I would love to hear (and share) your ethical stories. Please email me at: **sarah@sleepinglion.co.uk**.

Keep an eye on: **ethicalbusinessblog.com** for updates, case studies and further reading.

Sarah Duncan
Westminster, 2019

RESOURCES AND FURTHER READING

The body of literature on ethical and sustainable business practice is still relatively small but growing steadily. At the time of writing, I have read the main titles easily available. One-page summaries can be found at: ethicalbusinessblog.com. Do check back regularly as this library will continue to be updated after the publication of this book.

Authentic Marketing, Larry Weber
(John Wiley, 2019)

All In, David Grayson, Chris Coulter & Mark Lee
(Routledge 2018)

Brand Manners, Hamish Pringle & William Gordon
(Wiley, 2003)

Business Ethics, Andrew Crane & Dirk Matten
(Oxford University Press, 2010)

Clever, Rob Goffee & Gareth R Jones
(Harvard Business Review Press, 2009)

Compassion Inc, Gaurav Sinha
(Ebury Press, 2018)

Conscious Capitalism Field Guide, Raj Sisodia,
Timothy Henry & Thomas Eckschmidt
(Harvard Business Review Press, 2018)

Drive, Daniel Pink
(Canongate, 2011)

Engaging for success: enhancing performance through employee engagement, Macleod Report, 2012

Millennial Employee Engagement Study, Cone Communications, 2016

Natural Capital, Dieter Helm
(Yale University Press 2015)

No Bullshit Leadership, Chris Hirst
(Profile Books, 2019)

Sustainable Business: A One Planet Approach, Sally Jeanrenaud, Jean-Paul Jeanrenaud & Jonathan Gosling
(John Wiley, 2016)

The Ethical Capitalist, Julian Richer
(Random House, 2018)

The Five Dysfunctions of a Team, Patrick Lencioni
(John Wiley, 2002)

The Joy of Work, Bruce Daisley
(Random House, 2019)

The New Brand Spirit, Christian Conrad & Marjorie Ellis Thompson
(Gower Publishing, 2013)

The New Rules of Green Marketing, Jacquelyn Ottman
(Greenleaf, 2010)

The Pirate Inside, Adam Morgan
(John Wiley, 2004)

There is no Planet B, Mike Berners-Lee
(Cambridge University Press, 2019)

The Sales Person's Secret Code, Ian Mills, Mark Ridley,
Ben Laker & Tim Chapman
(LID, 2017)

The Sustainable Business, Jonathan T Scott
(Greenleaf, 2013)

WEconomy, Craig Kielburger, Holly Branson & Marc Kielburger
(John Wiley, 2018)

Why Should Anyone Work Here?, Rob Goffee & Gareth Jones
(Harvard Business Review Press, 2015)

BCorporation.net

CarbonTrust.com

Defra.gov.uk

HeyGirls.co.uk

Interface.com

Mindfulchef.com

Salesforce.org

TheSRA.org

Toms.co.uk

UN.org/sustainabledevelopment

ACKNOWLEDGMENTS

Many thanks for the wise comments and amazing endorsements from Mark Earls, Jon Khoo, Giles Gibbons, Peter Hancock, Stephan Loerke, Dr Sally Marlow, Fergus Boyd, Steven Day, Paul Edwards, Marjorie Ellis Thompson, Chris Hirst, Richard Morris, Hamish Pringle, Mark Smith, Kaye Taylor, Ceri Tinley and Kate Thompson.

Thanks also for the kind words of support from Andrew White (Triggerfish PR), Cameron Wilson (EcoAct) and Jane Pendlebury (HOSPA). Plus a big shout out to Sara Marshall for all her loveliness and constant encouragement.

To my amazing and talented stepdaughters, Rosie and Shaunagh: I cannot thank you enough for your enthusiasm, insights and invaluable contributions to this book.

And finally, my love and thanks go to my husband Kevin, for being just all round bloody marvellous.

The world is a better place with you people in it.

ABOUT THE AUTHOR

SARAH DUNCAN is a business development consultant and trainer. She has been in business for over 30 years – starting with luxury hotels, then moving through private club and spa development in Asia, to setting up her own consultancy, Sleeping Lion, in 2005. She has watched with interest as sustainability has forced its way onto the agenda, driven collectively by more ethically conscious employees and customers.

She now provides consultancy and workshops on ethical and responsible behaviour.

Contact the author for advice, training or speaking opportunities:

sarah@sleepinglion.co.uk
@sleepinglion
ethicalbusinessblog.com
sleepingliononline.com